WITHDRAWN

HOLOCAUST BIOGRAPHIES

Pastor André Trocmé
Spiritual Leader
of the French Village
Le Chambon

Allison Stark Draper

THE ROSEN PUBLISHING GROUP, INC.
NEW YORK

Published in 2001 by The Rosen Publishing Group, Inc.
29 East 21st Street, New York, NY 10010

Copyright © 2001 by The Rosen Publishing Group, Inc.

First Edition

Library of Congress Cataloging-in-Publication Data

Draper, Allison Stark
Pastor André Trocmé: spiritual leader of the French village Le Chambon / by Allison Stark Draper.—1st ed.
p. cm.—(Holocaust biographies)
Includes bibliographical references and index.
ISBN 0-8239-3378-4 (lib. bdg.)
1. Trocmé, André, 1901–1971—Juvenile literature. 2. Righteous Gentiles in the Holocaust—Biography—Juvenile literature. 3. World War, 1939–1945—Jews—Rescue—France—Le Chambon-sur-Lignon—Juvenile literature 4. Holocaust, Jewish (1939–1945)—France—Juvenile literature. 6. Le Chambon-sur-Lignon (France)—Ethnic relations—Juvenile literature.
[1. Trocmé, André, 1901–1971. 2. Righteous Gentiles in the Holocaust—Biography. 3. World War, 1939–1945—Jews—Rescue—France—Le Chambon-sur-Lignon. 4. Holocaust, Jewish (1939–1945)—France. 5. Jews—France—Le Chambon-sur-Lignon—History. 6. Le Chambon-sur-Lignon (France)—History. 7. France—History—German Occupation, 1940–1945.]
I. Title II. Series.
D804.66.T76 D73 2001
940.53'18'092—dc21

                                                          2001000182

Manufactured in the United States of America

Contents

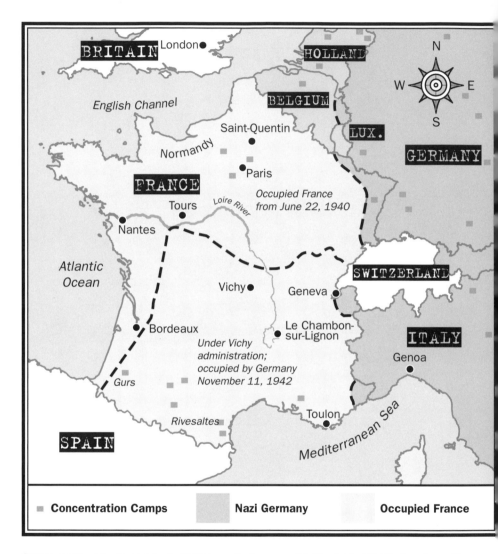

BRITAIN London●

English Channel

HOLLAND

BELGIUM

LUX.

N
W ● E
S

GERMANY

Saint-Quentin ●

Normandy

● Paris

FRANCE

Loire River

Occupied France
from June 22, 1940

Tours ●

● Nantes

Atlantic
Ocean

SWITZERLAND

Vichy ●

Geneva ●

● Bordeaux

Le Chambon-
sur-Lignon ●

ITALY

Under Vichy
administration;
occupied by Germany
November 11, 1942

Genoa
●

Gurs

Rivesaltes

Toulon
●

Mediterranean Sea

SPAIN

■ **Concentration Camps**   **Nazi Germany**   **Occupied France**

This map of occupied France between 1940 and 1942—during the
Vichy administration—shows the Nazi concentration camps and the
village of Le Chambon-sur-Lignon.

Introduction

Between 1939 and 1945, in the midst of one of the most terrible wars the world has ever known, the sheltered French villagers of Le Chambon saved the lives of 5,000 strangers. The farmers and villagers regarded what they did as simply human, claiming that it was what anyone would have done, that it was "normal." In the best of all worlds, it would have been normal, but during Word War II, when atrocity existed side by side with ordinary behavior, the town's actions were exceptional.

Le Chambon-sur-Lignon is one of several Protestant villages on the Plateau Vivarais-Lignon in the Haute-Loire region of France. During World War II, thousands of refugees, many of them Jews, found shelter there.

For the most part, the people of Le Chambon had little education or perspective on world events. What they did have was faith in their moral convictions and a deep trust in the word of God. They also had a leader, a Protestant pastor and conscientious objector named André Trocmé. He and his fellow pastor, Édouard Theis, were both determined pacifists. The day after France signed an armistice agreement with Nazi Germany in the early stages of World War II, they preached to the Chambonnais that it was the duty of Christians to use spiritual weapons to resist violence. This also meant to resist and disobey orders that were contrary to the orders of the Gospel. Ultimately, this meant facing and resisting the Nazis at the risk of imprisonment, torture, and death. André told them to act as Christians: without fear, but also without pride or hate.

The driving force of World War II was Germany's Nazi party under the leadership of Adolf Hitler, the chancellor of Germany.

Hitler's desire for world domination was second only to his desire to rid the world of Jews. Toward this end, he implemented laws forcing Jews to identify themselves as such, drove them out of public life, interned them in concentration camps, and murdered them in firing lines and gas chambers. Hitler did this over a period of time. First, Jews were made to sew yellow stars onto their clothing and hang signs saying "Jewish business" in their shop windows. Then they lost their jobs. Finally, they were arrested by police officers and deported.

The Nazis discouraged individualism and stressed the need for unquestioning obedience—to fathers, husbands, civil authorities, political leaders, and to Germany, the "Fatherland." The human virtue that Hitler most treasured was total submission. There was no room in his world for anyone who was "different" in any way— such as gays, free-thinkers, or Jews—nor was there any room for anyone who offered protection to these people. If captured, defenders of Hitler's victims became victims themselves. But Hitler's desire for absolute submission met its match in the tiny French village of Le Chambon-sur-Lignon. While leaders and religious organizations all over Europe caved in to the Nazi presence, and others the world over ignored or denied Hitler's vicious treatment of the Jews, the people of Le Chambon resisted courageously.

1. Resistance at Le Chambon-sur-Lignon

Le Chambon was an appropriate location for what was to become a scene of profound moral resistance. The village had been a stronghold for Protestants in the middle of Catholic France for more than 400 years, beginning with the Huguenots, Protestant followers of John Calvin.

During the sixteenth and seventeenth centuries, Catholic kings cruelly persecuted the Protestant people of France. Many fled to England and America. In 1529, the Protestant pastor of Le Chambon, Larent Chazot, was burned alive for his preaching. More than a century later—but nearly 300 years before André Trocmé preached nonviolence to the people of Le Chambon—the south of France was torn by violent battles between the Catholics and the Huguenots.

By the onset of World War II, most of the people who lived in and around Le Chambon were Protestant Christians, many of them descendents of the original Huguenots. The Chambonnais drew strength from their long history of resistance. They believed that it was wrong to force people to change their

This seventeenth-century French drawing depicts the St. Bartholomew's Day Massacre in Paris during which Roman Catholic mobs slaughtered thousands of Protestants.

religious faith. This belief made them tolerant and gave them the ability to question authority. They understood that a human authority figure could be wrong, a leader could be wrong, and a law could be wrong. For most of the Chambonnais, the highest authority, and only true moral and ethical guide was God.

In the Bible, one learns two of the lessons that the Chambonnais took most seriously: not to kill, and to love one's neighbor. The Bible also teaches that Jesus Christ was a Jew. The Old Testament, which is the first part of the Bible, describes God's creation of the world and the history of the Jewish people. The New Testament tells of the birth of Jesus and his teachings. Jews study the Old Testament, Protestants study both, and Catholics tend to focus on the New Testament. Many devout Protestant Chambonnais may have felt closer to the Jewish roots of their Christianity because they studied the Old Testament of the Bible.

André referred to Jews as the people of God. Some Jews who sought refuge in Le Chambon were startled by the friendly welcome they received. One German Jewish refugee recalled visiting an isolated farmhouse to buy eggs. The woman of the house asked if she was a Jew. Answering nervously that she was, the refugee almost took flight when the Frenchwoman turned to call to her husband. But the woman simply wanted her family to meet a Jew, one of the true people of God.

The Sanctity of Life

On Easter Sunday in 1901, André Pascal Trocmé was born in the French city of Saint-Quentin. His father, Paul Eugène Trocmé, was a Protestant businessman and a descendent of the Huguenots. André's mother, Paula Schwerdtmann, was German by birth and ancestry. She was also a devout Protestant. From the first moment of his life, André's parents hoped their son would grow up to be a pastor.

André's father was a wealthy man. His company made lace—a fine craft—in areas of northern France and neighboring Belgium. Because of his father's money and position in society, André grew up in a large house with a garden.

As a young boy, André studied with tutors rather than attending school. He had very little contact with the people of Saint-Quentin. André understood that his father's wealth made him "special," but he disliked the coldness associated with the upper classes. He felt more at home with his mother's German relatives who were more affectionate.

When André was ten, he took a car trip to the country with his parents, his brothers, and a cousin. Early in the trip, Paul Trocmé found himself trapped on a narrow road behind a smaller, slower car. He became frustrated with its pace and decided to pass. His wife protested his speed, but he ignored her—and then it was too late. The cars collided in a crunch of metal. André's father, brothers, and cousin were stunned and shaken. His mother had been thrown some distance from the car and was badly injured. Three days later, she died.

To André, the loss of his mother was almost unbearable. More than anything, he felt that the violent and horrific manner of her death was contrary to the spirit of Christianity. He began to understand that life was a fragile gift. It needed to be protected. This did not mean only one's own life or the lives of loved ones, it meant any life, whether that life belonged to a family member, a friend, another Protestant, or—as happened thirty years later in the town of Le Chambon—a Jew. From this point on, André's philosophy began to develop. From the age of ten, his understanding of the sacredness of life embraced all people and cemented his opposition to the evils of racial, political, and religious intolerance.

World War I

André's privileged childhood ended with the ravages of World War I. By 1914, his home in Saint-Quentin was occupied by German troops. Barbed wire surrounded the city, inhabitants could not travel without special permits, and there was little food. André's refuge during this time was a Protestant organization of young people called the Union of Saint-Quentin. The group conducted services, read the Bible, and prayed. They struggled against teenage temptations such as drinking and sexual adventure, as well as the more complex wartime desire to embrace hate and violence.

With the other members of this group, André engaged in his first resistance activities. Within the guarded city limits of Saint-Quentin, the Germans were forcing Russian prisoners to build underground bunkers. Many of the Russian prisoners were too weak and sick for heavy labor. When one fell at his task, a German soldier either kicked him until

A German soldier ties up a Russian prisoner
during World War I.

he got up, or shot him. André's group was horrified by the behavior of the German soldiers and by the starved state of the Russian prisoners. They decided to deliver food to the imprisoned workers. These activities were strictly against German law and each union member risked an eight-day prison sentence.

It was hard not to hate the Germans. André struggled with the idea that war itself was evil and not the German soldiers who had occupied his city. Ironically, it was a German soldier who introduced young André to the idea of conscientious objection. A conscientious objector is a person who refuses to participate in fighting and killing during times of war. This German soldier performed his job in the field as a telegrapher, but refused to carry weapons during battle. André saw that it was possible to resist fighting and refuse to do harm to others, even during war.

Five years later, in 1921, when André himself was a soldier in the French army, he chose not to take his rifle on a mission to map an area of Morocco. When his lieutenant discovered that André had left his weapon behind, he chastised André for endangering the other men in the party. André realized that he needed to make his position clearly known at the outset of a situation. By doing so, he could provide strength and inspiration to others. If he did not make his position clear, he realized that others might be harmed. André believed that to live by one's principles, one must declare them—to family, to friends, to colleagues, and even to governments.

Magda

When the war ended, André moved to Paris with his family. He studied theology at the University of Paris and joined an organization for nonviolence called the Fellowship of Reconciliation. In his spare time, he worked with young Protestants in the Union of Saint-Quentin. At school, he met a man named Édouard Theis. Years later, when André began his work in Le Chambon, he would recall Édouard's quiet strength, intelligence, and devotion to God. Later he would invite Édouard to join him in Le Chambon as a pastor and director of a new school.

While studying in Paris, André was offered a scholarship to the Union Theological Seminary in New York City. The seminary taught Social Gospel, focusing on social ills like poverty and lack of education. André admired and supported the people who shared a desire to improve the human condition. However, he was disheartened by the Social Gospel's lack of connection with God. The doctrine emphasized the here and now, at the expense of the spiritual life. While André saw the value and the legitimacy of a focus on practical realities, he believed it was meaningless to "put aside" spiritual issues to grapple with everyday problems. For André, there was no life without God.

In 1925, André tutored French to the children of John D. Rockefeller Jr. During this time, he often ate in the cafeteria of the International House in New York. One day, he met an Italian woman named Magda Grilli. As the days passed, he began looking forward to seeing and speaking with her. They took long walks and talked about their beliefs. Magda had grown up Catholic in Florence, Italy. She no longer considered herself Catholic—or Protestant, for that matter—because she thought religious groups confused the spiritual nature of religion. She believed that true religious life was about loving and caring for other human beings.

André worried that his intention to become a Protestant pastor and his desire to live a simple life might displease Magda. He need not have worried; from the beginning there was a deep connection between them. When André proposed to Magda, on April 18, 1926, she said yes at once. They immediately moved to France, to the parish of Maubeuge, a northern industrial city.

One year later, after the birth of their daughter, Nelly, they moved again, to the mining town of Sin-le-Noble, near the Belgian border. They spent six years in Sin-le-Noble, talking, praying, and offering guidance as well as advice to the miners. During that time, André and Magda had three sons —Jean-Pierre, Jacques, and Daniel. In 1934, the Trocmés were sent to the parish of Le Chambon.

Le Chambon-sur-Lignon

Le Chambon-sur-Lignon is a small village on the Lignon River in the midst of woods and fields. It sits unprotected on the southeastern corner of the Plateau du Velay. The buildings of Le Chambon were made from the drab granite of the surrounding countryside. During the nine long months of Le Chambon's winter, the swirling wind howls through the stone streets.

Although in 1934 Le Chambon was surrounded by farmland, the economy was supported mainly by tourism. Wealthy northerners spent the summer months living in hillside villas, walking in the woods, and

A view of the French village Le Chambon-sur-Lignon

fishing in the Lignon River. For the rest of the year, the town survived quietly.

To the energetic and affectionate Trocmés, there seemed to be an air of pessimism about the place. They were urban people—cultured and cosmopolitan. André and Magda had lived in France, Italy, Belgium, and the United States, and had traveled all over Europe. By comparison, Le Chambon was unsophisticated, sleepy, and taciturn. Still, the village and its people intrigued André. He knew of Le Chambon's history as a Protestant refuge for the Huguenots and admired the will of the people who had kept Protestantism so strong in such a tiny backwater. When André began to speak with the Chambonnais, he learned that they had a rock-solid faith. In a letter to an American friend, he wrote that in the town of Le Chambon, "the old Huguenot spirit is still alive. The humblest peasant home has its Bible and the father reads it every day. These people who do not read the papers but the Scriptures, do not stand on the moving soil of opinion but on the rock of the Word of God."

The Trocmés' house in Le Chambon was the presbytery, the section of the church reserved for clergymen and their families. Set on the main road, the Rue de la Grande Fontaine, the large stone building was the fifteenth-century summer house of the Comte de Fay. Its entrance led out to a courtyard that overlooked the Lignon River. The ground floor of the house included a large kitchen, a room that André used as his study, and a dining room with a view of the river and the peak of an extinct volcano called Le Mézenc. There were five bedrooms on the second floor, and a cavernous attic on the third. The Trocmés brightened the place at once despite strict wartime rationing restricting food and supplies. They filled the house with furniture, fabrics, flowers, a piano upon which Nelly played Mozart, and a parakeet in a birdcage.

Once they were settled, the Trocmés set out to meet the townspeople. André approached

Pastor Trocmé poses with a group of refugee children
in the village of Le Chambon-sur-Lignon.

this challenge with determination—there were 3,000 inhabitants in Le Chambon. André struggled to find a project that would unite and inspire all of them. After discussing and discarding some rather extreme possibilities—like building a toy factory—he decided to build a school.

The Cévenol School, as it was called, would be private, separate from the Le Chambon

Pastor André Trocmé (left) poses with Pastor Édouard Theis (right), whom he chose to run the Cévenol School, and Roger Darcissac at the entrance of the church in Le Chambon.

public school, and free from the rules of the French system. He hoped that the school's high standards and the same beautiful forests, fields, and mountains that attracted tourists would bring students and teachers from all over the world. Most important, the school would teach a philosophy of nonviolence and peace to students who could then carry their own ethic of goodness and tolerance into the world.

André needed a person to oversee the school. He wanted someone intelligent, devout, and capable. His first choice was Édouard Theis, his old friend. In the years since their time at the university, Édouard had taught in the United States, Madagascar, and Cameroon. Like André, Édouard was a conscientious objector.

Édouard agreed to come to Le Chambon in 1938, and André made him director of the school. Édouard ran the school, taught French, Latin, and Greek, and worked as a pastor at the church. There were four teachers, including Magda and Édouard's wife, Mildred, both of

whom worked for free. Slowly, the Cévenol
School grew. It became known both as an
institution of learning and as a place of safety
for refugees.

2. World War II

While André was building the Cévenol School
and his relationship with the people of Le
Chambon, the power of the German dictator
Adolf Hitler was growing steadily. Hitler's Nazi
Germany loomed dangerously to the north and
east of France. Hitler was obsessed with
"scientific" racism—or eugenics—the study
that deals with the control of human mating.
He believed that the Germans' ancestors, or
Aryans, belonged to a "master race."

Nazi Germany

The fact that Hitler rose to power was due, in
part, to the low morale of the German people
in the 1920s and 1930s. Germany had been
badly defeated in World War I, was deeply in

debt, and had lost territory by the signing of the Treaty of Versailles, the peace agreement drawn up to end the war. Many Germans believed that this settlement was unjust.

Between 1918 and 1924, the German economy collapsed. Several very conservative political parties began to grow, one of which was the Nazis. In the elections of 1928, the Nazis won 800,000 votes—only 2.6 percent. In

The *Sturmabteilung* (SA) or Brownshirts—the predecessors to Hitler's SS—block access to Jewish shops during a boycott in April 1933.

1930, they won 6.4 million. By 1932, Nazism was Germany's second largest political party. In 1933, Hitler became the chancellor, or prime minister, of Germany. Six years later, in September of 1939, Hitler's military forces invaded Poland, starting World War II.

Hitler proclaimed a "Thousand-Year Reich"—a projected timeframe in which the Nazis would win the war, conquer Europe, and rule the world. Part of the plan included the implementation of the Final Solution—the extermination of the Jewish people. By the end of the war, six million Jews had died, including one and a half million children. The Nazis also rounded up gays, people of the Roma and Sinti ethnic minorities, (commonly known as Gypsies), African Germans, and dissenters—people who resisted by saving Jews or by speaking out against Nazism.

Hitler claimed that his National Socialist German Workers' Party—or Nazi Party—offered Germans the chance to rise to the position of world power that they deserved. He advocated love of the Fatherland (Germany), discipline, patriotism, and an authoritarianism he believed would revive the economy and redefine Germany's political power.

Many Germans were enthusiastic about Hitler's ideas. Others disapproved. Nazism was antidemocratic; it sacrificed individual freedoms in favor of obedience to the government. It was misogynistic, maintaining that only men were fit for positions of authority in the world. Women were expected to remain at home and raise large families to increase the strength of the Fatherland. Also, Nazism was racist. In Hitler's Nazi propaganda, Aryans were blond, blue-eyed, healthy, and athletic. They were never of mixed blood. Most important, they were not Jewish.

Vichy, France

Hitler's forces invaded Poland on September 1, 1939. France and England declared war on Nazi Germany. For several months, there was a

German Jews

The presence of Jewish people in
Germany was not new. Jews had lived in
Germany and surrounding areas since
the time of the Roman Empire. Over the
course of 2,000 years, Jews had been
attacked by various governments,
forced to live in ghettos, and
penalized by discriminatory laws. By
the middle of the nineteenth century,
however, it seemed like the
persecution might finally come to an
end. German Jews were enjoying wealth,
success, and security.

In 1870, Jews won full civic
equality under German law and were
able to participate in government and
hold public office. Anti-Semitism had
not vanished, but it no longer seemed
like a real political danger. During
World War I, German Jews served their
country courageously and loyally. When
the war ended in 1918, people assumed
that Jewish life in Germany would
remain stable and safe.

German cavalry troops occupied Paris on June 14, 1940.

stalemate. Then German troops advanced into
the Netherlands and Belgium and into the
Ardennes, a forested region in France. The
French and British allies were surprised and
battered by a combined air and land attack,
known as blitzkrieg, or "lightning war."

On June 10, 1940, Italian forces joined the
Germans in the war. The French soldiers
fought courageously but hopelessly. They lost
almost 100,000 men. Four days later, the
Germans invaded Paris and France fell to the
Nazis. It had taken less than six weeks. The
Germans occupied northern France, including
Paris, from the Belgian border to the Loire
River. They also held the Atlantic seaboard.

A new French government was formed in the
unoccupied southeastern interior and
Mediterranean coast. This became known as the
Free Zone. The leader of unoccupied France was
Marshal Henri Philippe Pétain, a venerated,
eighty-four year old hero of World War I.

Pétain advocated what he called the
"National Revolution" which was intended to

bring about a new, more orderly, disciplined France—essentially a France more in line with Nazi Germany. Pétain's government was based in Vichy, a town in central France. Pétain was determined to cooperate with the Nazis. In speeches, he praised the ancient tradition of France and allied it with Nazism by highlighting such virtues as patriotism. Police punished resisters to his National Revolution. Less than four months after the Nazi occupation began, Pétain signed a decree that defined Jews under French law and banned them from holding public office or working in the mass media. Over time, he continued to increase restrictions for Jews in the areas of work, education, property ownership, and travel.

At the start of the occupation, Hitler expressed interest in a "collaboration" with the Vichy government. In fact, Germany's main interest was that the Vichy government should oppress the French people, keeping them quiet and productive. By the fall of 1943, in the fourth year of the German occupation,

The French Concentration Camps

Before the Vichy regime, the French
government had been relatively
liberal. France had been a land of
asylum, or refuge, for foreign Jews.
By 1940, half of the 350,000 Jews in
France were foreign-born. Under the
Vichy government, France ceased to be
a refuge.

French police rounded up Jews in
broad daylight in the streets of Paris
in 1941. Even before the German
occupation, the French government had
concentration camps used to house
political radicals, refugees, and common
criminals. These were not death camps,
but they were grim, ugly places
surrounded by barbed wire. The Vichy
government enlarged these camps and
used them for Jews and resisters. By
January of 1942, some 3,000 Jews had
died in these camps. In total, there
were forty-nine concentration camps, two
of which—Gurs and Rivesaltes—were in
the south, in the unoccupied free zone.

between 40 and 50 percent of the fruits of all French production—agricultural and industrial—was going to Germany. But manufactured goods and produce were not all that Nazi Germany wanted from France. They also wanted to kill the French Jews.

Mass arrests and deportations of Jews to Nazi death camps began in the summer of 1942. At first, the Nazis were disappointed with

Henri Philippe Pétain, French general and head of the pro-Nazi Vichy government, shakes hands with Hitler in October 1940.

the results. They wanted to completely fill the trains headed to the death camps. Pétain and the Vichy regime agreed to deliver Jews; foreign Jews especially, but French Jews as well. A government official named Pierre Laval suggested that it was better not to separate families and offered to send children, for whom the Nazis had not yet asked. Over the course of the war, France contributed more than 75,000 Jews, including 10,000 children, to the Nazi death total of twelve million.

The Seeds of Resistance

During the first year of the war, André and Édouard argued against France's decision to enter the war. After the Nazi occupation, they took the unpopular position that France should not collaborate with the Nazis. Many French citizens seemed to disagree with them, but the people of Le Chambon, along with their pastors, saw the essential immorality of collaboration. They realized that what Pétain described as France's "honorable" armistice with the Germans was, in fact, in the words of Le Chambon's public school director Roger Darcissac, an "armistice of dishonor." Through this armistice, Germany was imposing its fascist ideas on the French people. André and Édouard had nothing but contempt for Marshal Pétain and his ideas.

The Cévenol School began its third year under the shadow of the Vichy government. Pétain, with his emphasis on duty, obedience, and patriotism, issued a decree that all students in French schools must salute the French flag every morning before lessons—using the stiff-handed Nazi salute. Some teachers and students liked the idea. Others did not see any harm in it. For André, the salute order of the Vichy government provided a first opportunity for open resistance. André believed that the use of the fascist salute was the first step in the acceptance of Nazi rule. He refused to give the salute.

Such clear resistance was dangerous, not only for André himself, but for his students and their families. The resistance had to be handled cleverly enough to keep the authorities from questioning the students and faculty or from closing the school. The director of the public school across the street, Roger Darcissac, designed a plan. If he raised the flag in front of his school, the Cévenol students could stand across the street and salute or not as they saw fit. This way, Cévenol would still have apparent compliance with the law.

Since no one came from the government to monitor the flag ceremony, the students and teachers at both schools ceased to follow the law. Nonetheless, the flag incident was important. It demonstrated to every man, woman, and child in Le Chambon that nonviolent resistance was indeed possible. The Chambonnais had begun their fight.

Not long afterward, on August 1, 1941, Vichy officials ordered that the church bells in Le Chambon be rung in homage to Marshal Pétain

Entrance to the Protestant church in Le Chambon,
complete with the inscription "Love One Another"

for founding a militant group in the service of his National Revolution grounded in hatred of Jews, communists, and Freemasons. André asked the custodian of the church, a woman named Amélie, not to ring the bells for Pétain. A staunch Protestant and antifascist, Amélie also objected to the National Revolution and agreed.

The next day, André noticed the bells did not ring and was proud of Amélie's act of resistance. Only later did he find out that her resistance had been active rather than passive. Amélie had physically prevented two vacationing French women from entering the church and ringing the bells themselves.

A Letter to Vichy, France

Officials of the Vichy regime were not entirely blind to the pocket of resistance that existed in Le Chambon. In August of 1942, they sent their minister of youth, Georges Lamirand, and a prefect named Bach to visit. The two men arrived in uniform with a delegation expecting

the customary reception, followed by a parade, banquet, and religious services.

Lamirand and his group were usually greeted by cheering youth and excited townspeople. Instead, the village ignored the procession. The ministers were met with the dull granite of Le Chambon's narrow streets and an apathetic turnout. Surprised by the lack of interest, Lamirand gave only a brief speech. He ended it with a cry of "Long live Marshal Pétain!" Rather than responding in unison, the small crowd remained silent. A Salvation Army officer yelled, "Long live Jesus Christ!"

The villagers escorted the Vichy officials to the church for services. A visiting Swiss pastor preached the importance of obeying the state when obedience does not entail violating the laws of God. Then the congregation sang. One of the townspeople, Marie Brottes, recalled having felt so unified and strong while singing, that if the Nazis had arrived just then, the entire village would have lined up and fearlessly faced the Nazis' machine guns. When the services were finished, a group of older Cévenol students approached Lamirand. They handed him a letter describing a roundup of more than 28,000 Jews that had taken place in Paris shortly before. The letter stated that the policies of the Vichy government were unacceptable to the youth of Le Chambon.

The Roundups

Shortly after the Vichy visit, the chief of police of nearby Haute-Loire arrived to deport every Jew he could find as part of the Nazi *Nacht und Nebel* (Night and Fog) policy to exterminate the Jewish people. He demanded that André compile a list of the names of every Jew hiding in the town of Le Chambon so they could "register" at city hall. André refused. He said that he did not know their real names. (This was true; he had learned only the aliases of the Jewish refugees). He would not give them up even if he did know their names. He was their shepherd, and they were his flock.

45

He would not deliver them into the hands of evil. The chief of police was enraged.

That night, the children of Le Chambon ran from house to house, warning the refugees to scatter into the woods and hide. The next day, the police began to search in earnest. They entered houses, checked bedrooms, closets, cellars, and attics. They checked for hollowed walls. They searched barns, fields, and haylofts. They scrutinized identity papers, but they were too late. The refugees had disappeared into the countryside.

One Jew was arrested. His name was Stekler. The police placed him on a bus, where he sat alone. As he waited, Jean-Pierre Trocmé, the oldest son of the Trocmés, pushed a piece of chocolate through the window to him. Soon, despite the wartime rationing, almost everyone found some small gift to hand to Stekler through the window. Soon he sat surrounded by a pile of presents as police looked on in amazement.

After this inauspicious start, the French police arrested only one other person in Le

Chambon before they ended the roundups. As time passed, roundups of Jews and non-Germans became more frequent all over France. Roundups in Le Chambon were particularly unsuccessful because of the unwillingness of the villagers to betray their Jewish refugees to the Vichy government. The defiant spirit of Le Chambon sometimes had a contagious effect on the police.

One day, the son of the mayor of Le Chambon was reading under a tree. A police officer quietly approached the boy and advised him to "get lost." The officer continued, saying, "Just go. I haven't seen you." The boy realized that the officer thought he was a Jew and was trying to save his life. This contagion of goodness, or goodwill effect, continued to spread. By the time the Nazis finally arrived in Vichy, France, in November of 1942, there were often late-night "warning" calls to the Trocmés. And almost always, there would be a hunt for the Jewish refugees the following day.

3. The French Resistance

The Vichy government was a puppet government—the Vichy officials moved when the Nazis pulled the strings. It was a government submissive to the Nazi occupation and to Nazi policy. Some French people supported Pétain; others objected. But most people wanted to avoid the ravages of the Nazis, so they kept their opinions to themselves.

André Trocmé believed that this type of apathy added to the problem. To ignore wrongdoing enabled it to grow. Immoral behavior ends only when it is identified and actively resisted. Some French people actively resisted. At the one end of the spectrum was the nonviolent resistance of André Trocmé and the citizens of Le Chambon, who were opposed to death, even that of a

German soldier. Their position was not typical. Much of the organized French Resistance did not support nonviolence. As people across France found the acts and policies of the Nazis weighing upon their consciences, they created separate cells of resistance, some of which grew into armed forces.

The Beginning of Opposition

The beginnings of resistance were already visible in the summer of 1940, after France suffered its defeat. French general Charles de Gaulle established a government-in-exile in London. In radio broadcasts, he addressed the people of France, urging them to back him in the ongoing fight against the Germans. De Gaulle had the support of British Prime Minister Winston Churchill, who never wavered in his stand against Hitler and the Nazi party.

French patriots in occupied France cut telephone lines servicing the Germans, destroyed goods bound for Germany, painted anti-Nazi graffiti on public walls, and helped escaped prisoners of war flee to England and other safe havens. Resistance radio networks kept the British posted on the activities of the occupying Germans.

During 1941, as more countries became involved in the war, the French received international support and the Resistance grew.

Charles de Gaulle set up a French government-in-exile in London and actively encouraged the French Resistance.

There were bombings in Nantes, Bordeaux, and Paris. Each success of the Resistance provoked swift and often vicious violence from the Vichy regime, as well as massive executions of French prisoners by the Germans. Despite the punishments, Resistance efforts continued.

The Secret Army and the Maquis

During the winter of 1942–1943, the German army forced the Vichy government to hand over its weapons. The Germans then sank the French fleet off the coast of Toulon. Many of the French soldiers who had been preparing to fight for the Vichy government now fled to the Resistance. The Germans, who were beginning to suffer defeats at the hands of the Allied forces (Great Britain, the Soviet Union, and the United States), needed more men to fight and to fulfill the growing demand for manual labor.

They tried to send young French men to Germany for forced labor, but found them extremely reluctant to go. Some obtained medical excuses. Others went into hiding in the *maquis* (forests) of France. The men and women hiding in the forests became known as *maquisards,* or members of the French Resistance movement called the Maquis. Both the Maquis and the Secret Army of General Charles de Gaulle wanted to free France from the Nazis and from the puppet

Two members of the Maquis, a group of French Resistance fighters, are shown how to care for a carbine rifle.

government of Marshal Pétain in Vichy by means of violence.

Resistance Fighters in Le Chambon

André Trocmé was completely opposed to the violent methods of both sects of the French Resistance—the Secret Army and the Maquis—but he sympathized with their positions. André knew many of the local members of both groups, spoke with them about their methods, and tried to dissuade them from acts of violence. The Resistance fighters applauded André's efforts, but believed that strong action—and sometimes violence—was necessary. They did not only want to remove the Jews from harm's way; they wanted to drive the invading Germans from French soil. During the last weeks of the war, the Chambonnais benefited from the militant approach of the Resistance fighters who protected the village by driving off bands of German marauders.

André's relations with the members of the Resistance were based on the mutual respect between him and the leader of the local Secret Army. Together the men spent a great deal of time debating the Secret Army's methods.

Less extreme than the Maquis, the Secret Army still advocated a violence that André could not accept. Despite differences in their views, however, the two men discussed the tactical necessities of protecting Le Chambon and ensuring the preservation of life in the surrounding area. The citizens of Le Chambon not only offered shelter to Jewish refugees, but also provided farms and safe houses for Resistance fighters dodging German soldiers.

The Maquis were younger and less disciplined than the Secret Army. Some were former Cévenol students who had become frustrated with André's nonviolent methods and wanted to take a more active role against the Germans. The maquisards were brave and passionate, but sometimes foolish. They sometimes behaved as though the supplies and stores of Le Chambon were at their disposal. They took without asking—cars, motorcycles, food, tools, and weapons. Some of the Secret Army leaders stationed near Le Chambon became so exasperated with the maquisards that they were ready to shoot them for looting.

Léon Eyraud, a member of the Le Chambon community, bridged the gap between the nonviolent resistance of his village and the militant activities of the Resistance fighters.

Léon's wife, Antoinette, ran one of Le Chambon's safe houses, and Leon acted as a contact point for local intelligence. When military supplies were delivered to the area, Léon was informed of the precise location. Léon used the code name *Père Noël,* or "Father Christmas"; Noël is Léon spelled backwards. He also kept track of the movements of German military personnel in the area. Léon believed that some level of armed conflict was inevitable in war and it was best to be prepared. His personal conscience, however, abhorred unnecessary death and guided him to act without violence.

When the Nazis moved into southern France in 1942, they set up their Le Chambon headquarters directly across the street from Léon and Antoinette's home, taking over two hotels and filling them with wounded soldiers. Jews, resisters, and maquisards came and went constantly from the Eyrauds' safe house. These comings and goings were so obvious that it is difficult to understand why the Nazi soldiers took no action.

According to the hotelkeeper, when the Germans first arrived in Le Chambon, the soldiers would return from their walks in the woods and tell him, "The woods are full of Jews!" He would answer, "Those aren't Jews! They're tourists!" The Germans would look at him in disbelief, and walk away. The Eyrauds' daughter thought that the injured soldiers may have been happy just to be at peace, away from the fighting at the front. They may also have been infected by the quiet spirit of antiviolence in Le Chambon.

Saving the Children

Magda Trocmé's first unannounced German Jewish refugee arrived on the doorstep of the presbytery in the winter of 1940–1941. Soon, Le Chambon was an official safe haven for Jews. As more people came seeking help and hiding places, André decided to establish an official connection with the resistance effort.

The Quakers

André contacted the Quakers, an American religious society dedicated to nonviolence. The Quakers were in France, bringing food and supplies to prisoners. They had won the trust of the Vichy government and were allowed to take provisions to war victims and starving children in the south of France. Like André, the Quakers believed it was not enough merely to resist violence; one was responsible for lessening or ending the suffering of others, whenever possible. The Quakers' convictions regarding the sacredness of life, the importance of the individual, and the religious obligation to

Henri Couvot (center), head of the American Friends Service Committee in Aspet, France, poses with a group of Jewish children who were rescued from French transit camps in 1941.

love one's neighbors were similar to André's. André wanted to meet with the Quakers.

André met with Burns Chalmers. Burns knew about André's strong stance against violence and his ability as a leader and orator, to inspire people. Burns believed that André was more effective in Le Chambon than if he volunteered his services to the Quakers. Burns remarked on the unusual security that Le Chambon provided for refugees, given its location, dense forests, and its laconic townspeople. Together, Burns and André agreed that Le Chambon might do the greatest good by saving children; providing a safe, healthy, ethical environment for young people was one of the reasons André had begun to establish the Cévenol School.

Burns told André that the Quakers were providing prisoners with false medical certificates, declaring them unfit for deportation. They tried to save both fathers and mothers; if they failed, they took responsibility for the children. The difficulty came in locating enough families willing to risk harboring Jewish children. André believed that Le Chambon could provide the children with homes, schooling, and security. Burns offered to supply funds to manage a house of refuge.

Although André was the pastor of Le Chambon, and the people of his parish trusted him, he could not make the decision to turn Le Chambon into a safe haven by himself. When he returned from his meeting with Burns Chalmers, he called a council. He presented the idea of hiding and protecting children who needed help, but whose presence would gravely endanger the village.

Without the support of the villagers, the plan could not succeed. André's leadership and spiritual influence led to the unanimous agreement of the council. With their pervasive spirit of good will, they vowed to dedicate themselves to saving children.

André named his cousin, Daniel
Trocmé, as director of two refugee
homes in Le Chambon during the war.

The Safe Houses

Once the townspeople agreed, they set up
several safe houses directed by different relief
organizations. One of the first, called the
Crickcts, was an old boardinghouse located a
few miles from the center of Le Chambon.
André appointed his cousin, Daniel Trocmé,
as its director.

Daniel was a teacher of languages, history, and geography. As the director of the Crickets, it was his job to feed, clothe, protect, and educate the children. True to his word, Burns Chalmers and the Quakers sent money to help with the cost of food, clothing, and supplies, even after the Quakers left the region.

The Crickets was the first of several safe houses. Daniel also directed another refuge called the House of the Rocks. A third haven was the Farm School, funded by the Swiss. Established to teach modern farming techniques to farmers and children, its country location made it an important place of refuge. Those who stayed there were protected by the panoramic view the house afforded—no one could approach the building or structure unseen—and by the loud barking of dogs, who were alert to the presence of any movement on the country roads.

One of the most important havens in Le Chambon was the Cévenol School. Many of its ranks of both students and teachers were

Daniel Trocmé directed the House of the Rocks, a refuge
for older students in Le Chambon.

refugees. One of these teachers was a man named Daniel Isaac, a Frenchman and a Protestant. Daniel found himself marked as a Jew in France's newly anti-Semitic climate because he had Jewish grandparents.

When André invited him to Cévenol one summer session to teach philosophy, Daniel initially refused. André convinced him, emphasizing that Daniel would be doing a favor for Le Chambon. At last he agreed and taught the summer session. In the fall, when Daniel left Le Chambon to fight for the Resistance, his wife and children decided to remain. Daniel later remarked that while André had made it seem that he would be helping Le Chambon and Cévenol, it was André who was offering protection to Daniel and his family before they even realized that they needed it. As always, André was aggressively engaged in saving lives.

4. Eye of the Storm

By this time, André and Magda Trocmé were
hiding some refugees in their home and assisting
in the rescue of others, setting an example of
compassion for other villagers to follow. When
new refugees arrived in Le Chambon in need of
shelter, André would announce to the
congregation, "Three Old Testaments have
arrived"—a code phrase that let the church
members know that three "Old Testaments," or
Jews, needed a place to hide. For every new arrival,
someone would stand up and say, "I'll take them."

The Underground Railroad

Le Chambon was not only a refuge; it was also a
way station. In the same way the Underground

Railroad developed in the United States before the Civil War to help slaves in their flight to freedom, European way stations helped Jews on their way to Switzerland or America. As the persecution of the Jews worsened, word spread about Le Chambon—one of several French villages that resisted the Nazis.

The Chambonnais provided more than just shelter. Roger Darcissac, the public school director, made false identification cards for those whose Jewish names prevented them from crossing borders. The forgers of Le Chambon also made false ration cards, enabling refugees to purchase food.

The arrival of a particularly skillful forger, a Jewish teenager who went by the French name Jean-Claude Plunne, turned Le Chambon into a major center for the manufacture and distribution of false papers. Plunne himself turned out papers for fifty people each week.

Plunne lived with Henri and Emma Héritier. The Héritiers knew Plunne was Jewish, and a forger, though they never spoke of it. As forgery was one of the most punishable crimes, it was extremely dangerous to have false papers in the house. Henri suggested to Plunne that he hide the papers in some old beehives in the woods. Later, they moved the papers to a box that they kept under the earth near Henri's mother's grave. Plunne estimated that there were probably 5,000 Jews living in and hiding in the village of Le Chambon, doubling the population of the town.

The Refugees

Not all of the refugees in Le Chambon were Jewish. There were also anti-Nazi Germans who left Germany and Austria to avoid living under Nazi law. Young Frenchmen escaping forced labor camps in Germany came through town on their way to join the Maquis. Even the French Jews—many of whom were shocked to be persecuted by their own government and surprised to think of themselves as "Jewish" instead of French—were now refugees. The majority, however, were foreign Jews. Many were eastern Europeans who had experienced anti-Semitism all their lives. Others were German Jews who thought of themselves as German and felt betrayed by their own government.

Many of the refugees who stayed for more than a few days worked hard to make themselves useful in the village. Two of them

Many of the refugees who passed through Le Chambon—such as the elderly French couple pictured here—were non-Jews.

lived at the presbytery with the Trocmés for the duration of the war. One of them, Madame Grünhut—known as Madame Berthe—cooked for the Trocmés. The other, a cabinetmaker named Monsieur Kohn, alias Monsieur Colin, made furniture and did repairs around the house. Other refugees taught, worked with the Red Cross, did odd jobs, or assisted the two very overworked doctors of the town.

The Arrest

Helping the refugees was a dangerous business for André Trocmé and the villagers. It was dangerous in an additional way for André Trocmé, Édouard Theis, and Roger Darcissac. Leaders are easily identified by an enemy, and often accept a greater level of moral responsibility. André met this challenge three years into the Nazi occupation of France. In February 1943, a black car pulled in front of the presbytery and two Vichy police officers stepped out. The first was Major Silvani, the chief of police for Haute-Loire—a different chief from the man who had taken Stekler. The second was his lieutenant. When Silvani knocked on the Trocmés' door, André was away visiting parishioners. Magda opened the door and let the officers into André's office. Then she returned to the kitchen and braced herself. André returned two hours later. When he emerged from his office, he announced to Magda that he was being arrested.

Magda invited the officers to join them for dinner; they accepted. André enjoyed what might be his last good meal. While they ate, neighbors and villagers heard of the arrest and came in to say good-bye. They were sad, angry, or resigned. Many of them wept. Almost all of them pressed small gifts upon André, knowing the deprivations of prison to be far worse than the rationing of wartime life. He found himself with a heap of such luxuries as candles, canned sardines, chocolates, sausage, socks, and toilet paper. The officers were amazed by this affection and felt shamed by their task. When someone asked how André would light the candles, Silvani offered his own matches.

After dinner, Silvani and his lieutenant took André to the car and informed him that they were also arresting Édouard Theis and Roger Darcissac. Silvani did not know the charges. Each of the men knew the extent of his activities and feared the worst.

Édouard was also a conscientious objector. He and André had been in complete agreement regarding resistance. Roger, who directed the public school in Le Chambon, had been involved in forging documents and sheltering Jews. When new students arrived, he registered them with whatever names they gave him. He never pressed them for information and always denied their Jewish heritage when questioned by the authorities.

The three men were taken to the concentration camp of Saint-Paul d'Eyjeaux. The camp consisted of a group of low wooden barracks surrounded by a double row of high, barbed-wire fences. Soldiers stood in the guard towers holding machine guns. The prisoners were fingerprinted and photographed. Their possessions were taken and their noses were measured in order to test whether they were Jewish—a ridiculous exercise that was the Vichy government's anti-Semitic contribution to Nazism.

The camp was grim. Even André felt afraid at the sight of it. Inside, there were about 500

Pastors Édouard Theis *(left)* and André Trocmé lead a discussion at the camp of Saint Paul d'Eyjeaux.

political prisoners. They were thin, dirty, and sarcastic. André thought their sarcasm was a good sign. It meant that their spirits were not yet broken by the hardships they had suffered.

Following their instincts to teach and lead, André, Édouard, and Roger organized religious discussions within the camp. Their Protestant services were well-attended. As most of the prisoners were Jewish, Catholic, or atheist, the camp director became concerned. He stationed a police officer at the meetings. André, Édouard, and Roger developed a code for their sermons and discussions in which they substituted the name of Karl Marx—the father of communist philosophy—for the name of Marshal Pétain. This way they could denounce the Vichy government while the police officer believed they were describing the evils of communism. Soon, the hardened communists and war veterans began to recognize the value of the ideas preached in the sermons. André and his colleagues were turning the concentration camp into a learning center for moral conviction.

The Release

André, Édouard, and Roger had been in the camp at Saint-Paul d'Eyjeaux for more than a month when they were asked to report to the camp director. They were certain that the police officer had reported them for causing trouble. To their surprise, they discovered that they were being released. However, the release was conditional. They could leave only if they signed an oath agreeing to obey the orders of the Vichy government without question. Roger signed it without much concern. As a public school director, he had signed such documents before and knew that he would disregard the oath without moral qualms.

André and Édouard refused to sign. Édouard maintained that the oath was against his conscience. The camp director thought they were both insane—they were forsaking the opportunity to leave a concentration camp. But, the pastors had more than their own welfare to consider. They were teachers and religious leaders. It was their job to set an example by their own actions. Only true integrity could inspire the moral strength and good works of others. The director was at first exasperated, and then angry. He let Roger go and sent the religious men back to the barracks.

Amazingly, the next day, the director called for André and Édouard again. When they informed him that they were still unwilling to sign, he told them not to worry; he had orders to free them without signatures.

No one is quite sure why the men were freed. Some believe that the prefect, Bach, who visited Le Chambon with youth minister Lamirand, had claimed the number of Jews in Le Chambon was negligible. It may be that the ministers were released at his request. Others believe that the leaders of the French Protestant Church resented the Vichy

government's treatment of Protestant
ministers and may have spoken on the pastors'
behalf. It is also possible that the camp
director was concerned that André and
Édouard were inspiring the prisoners in some
subversive manner. Only days after the two
men left, the rest of the prisoners were
shipped to eastern European concentration
camps. The Nazis killed nearly all of them.

The Gestapo Raid

The people of Le Chambon were taking great
risks without regarding their actions as heroic
or abnormal. Their reluctance to view
themselves as brave or unusual did not make
their position any less dangerous. One of the
leaders of the Chambonnais resistance,
Daniel Trocmé, died for his convictions.

Daniel was the young cousin André
appointed to run the Crickets and the House of
the Rocks. Daniel was committed to saving the
lives of the refugee children. He cooked for

them, patched their clothes, resoled their shoes, listened to their fears, and used his well-read intellect to coach them in their studies. When he accepted the job, he wrote to his parents, "I have begun to become responsible to other people. Le Chambon is a noble place of contribution to the changes needed in our world. Only the future will explain if I was useful to these tasks or not. And it will be revealed only to me because my successes are small in the eyes of the world. I have chosen Le Chambon to rid my life of shame."

André described Daniel as both unselfish and ethical. It was this pure conscience that drove Daniel to accuse a Vichy police officer of neglecting his responsibility by loading a group of prisoners into a bus. This action may well have led to Daniel's death.

In the summer of 1943, the Gestapo raided the Crickets. They arrested Daniel and the children and took them to the House of the Rocks. One of Daniel's students, a young woman named Suzanne, slipped away and ran to the presbytery to warn Magda, who then rushed to the House of the Rocks.

When she arrived, she noticed three buses in front of the entrance. She immediately marched into the house and found Daniel's students sitting against the wall, faced by several armed Germans. Daniel was among them. The Germans had mistaken him for an older man who brought food to the house. Magda was apparently mistaken for a maid. She was ordered into the kitchen, where she and the cook prepared eggs for the officers. The Germans ate and then interrogated the young people. When the students emerged from the small room, some had bruises on their faces. As they passed Magda, they whispered messages to be passed on to their families or handed her the scribbled addresses of friends. They felt certain they would be deported.

After interrogating all of the students and Daniel, the Gestapo told Magda to give the prisoners some bread. While she was handing

A page from the journal of Peter Feigl, a German Jewish child who hid in Le Chambon. His parents, shown here, later perished in the camps.

out the bread, Daniel murmured to Magda that he had a plan. Several weeks earlier, a Spanish boy named Pepito had saved a German soldier from drowning in the Lignon River. Daniel suggested that Magda appeal to the Germans to spare the lives of the prisoners in return for this act. Magda set off for the German headquarters and found two German officers who knew of the rescue. She persuaded them to return with her to the House of the Rocks. When they arrived, Magda was able to introduce the soldiers to the Gestapo agents, raise the subject of Pepito, and secure the prisoners' release.

Later in the day, Magda returned to the House of the Rocks to see if Daniel and the other children had been released. Her oldest son, fourteen year old Jean-Pierre, insisted on going with her. They arrived to find Daniel standing at the head of a line of students, waiting to board one of the buses.

More than a year later, the Trocmés learned what had happened to Daniel. He had been interrogated repeatedly; the compassion he expressed for the Jews convinced his captors that he must himself be Jewish. Daniel Trocmé was gassed and incinerated at the Maidanek death camp in Poland on April 4, 1944. Thirty-two years later, in 1976, the State of Israel posthumously awarded Daniel Trocmé the Medal of Righteousness and a tree was planted in his memory.

The Spy

In 1942, Vichy leaders sent Commissioner Praly to Le Chambon to spy on the Maquis and the Jews. Praly was a young and charming Protestant who sat in the cafés of Le Chambon for hours, smiling at the Chambonnais and engaging them in conversation. His assignment was to use his skills of observation—as well as bribes and threats—to compile lists of names of the Jews and resistance fighters. He reported his findings to Vichy officials daily, in large envelopes that he sent by rail. There was no mystery about his reason for being in the village; Praly never pretended to be anything other than a Vichy agent. Like so many soldiers and officers in the village, he developed a relationship with André Trocmé and may have been influenced by André's moral conscience. Praly's reports, for instance, never led to an effective raid. Also, shortly before the Gestapo arrested Daniel Trocmé, Praly warned André that the House of the Rocks was under scrutiny.

Even so, the local Maquis did not trust Praly. They tolerated his presence in the village for almost a year. Then, in the summer of 1943, they decided to kill him. Four armed maquisards entered the village one evening. They approached the hotel where Praly lived. Two maquisards remained outside on guard while the other two entered the building. They found Praly in the dining room and asked him to step outside. When he did, they shot him dead and left his body in the hotel's hallway. André, who was angered and disgusted by their actions, never discovered the identities of the killers.

After Praly's murder, both Vichy and Nazi officials concentrated their attention on Le Chambon more actively and viciously than before. The Gestapo's raid on the House of the Rocks was only one instance of their anger. In a subtler move, the Gestapo tried to discourage the organized, nonviolent resistance that was occurring in Le Chambon by putting a price on the head of André Trocmé. André learned this from a maquisard who was acting as a double agent in the Gestapo. The agent warned André that the assassination would be a hit-and-run affair, thus preventing a public outcry against the killing of a man so widely beloved. He urged André to run.

André considered his options. He was useful to the resistance effort both as an individual and as a symbol. On the one hand, his death might be devastating to the morale of not only the people of Le Chambon, but of other French resisters as well. On the other hand, his flight might be seen as cowardice, or as a lack of conviction in his actions against the Nazis. André believed that part of his job as an advocate of nonviolence was to prove its power against atrocity. He wrestled with the question of whether to flee.

André needed the advice of others. One friend, who was an important Protestant official, advised flight. He pointed out that André's death—and the possible death of all the children in his charge—might prove too much for the villagers. They might lose faith and forsake their work for the refugees. In addition, the assassination might not take place when André was alone. It might also mean the deaths of Magda, the children, or other parishioners.

This seemed too great a chance for André to take. His responsibility was to save lives, not to expose them to avoidable risks. André remained undecided. He saw the value in all of these points, but he also worried that without him, the villagers would lose their leader and, therefore, might lose their faith. Finally, André reached the conclusion that a decision that would endanger his family was not the correct decision.

5. Escape and Deliverance

André waited for a sunny Sunday when it would be natural for him to bicycle out into the country with his family. They climbed onto their bicycles and headed east. Some distance from the village, André said good-bye and caught a ride with a hardware dealer. By evening, he was safe at the Protestant presbytery of Lamastre.

He had a ration card and a new identity. André stayed in the town until the enraged pastor of Lamastre returned from vacation and sent André on his way. As luck would have it, André narrowly avoided the Gestapo team that came looking for him in Lamastre. He found refuge first in a house in Ardèche and later in Drôme.

André did not curtail his work because members of the Gestapo were hunting him. He wrote long letters to Magda in which he discussed the progress of the resistance in Le Chambon. While he was in hiding, André's middle son, Jacques, came to live with him.

This was a very happy time for both father and son. They played and studied together, and focused on Jacques' education. When André had to attend an important meeting in Lyons, he took Jacques with him. On the way back, they were late for the train. André left Jacques on the platform and ran to the baggage house to collect their luggage. The next moment he was trapped by two German soldiers and shoved into a prison van.

As they could not know who he was, André assumed they had arrested him for running in the railway station. He called to the soldiers in fluent German, asking that they bring his son to him so that he could explain. The Nazis, who had believed André had been escaping a roundup—anyone running looked suspicious—saw that perhaps there had been a misunderstanding. They set André free, but followed him to the checkpoint where André's papers would be reviewed.

As he stood in line to have his papers examined, André realized three things. First, the last name on his false papers would not match the name on his son's. Second, the guard was checking papers against a pile of photographs of people wanted by the Gestapo. Third, and most important, to stand by the name on his false papers would be a lie.

To carry false papers was one thing; it gave sympathetic French officers a way to avoid exposing André to the Germans. To use them himself, to announce to another human being, "Yes, my name is Monsieur Béguet," would be, in the words of the Bible, to "bear false witness." André realized that he could not commit the sin of lying simply to save himself. But Jacques' life was also in danger. There was only one answer—André and Jacques would have to slip out of the station. André spoke quietly to Jacques, maneuvering himself and his son behind a pillar. When the soldier looked away, André and Jacques strolled quietly and unhurriedly out of the station. No one saw them go. Father and son walked through the streets of Lyons until they found a Protestant church. They entered, knelt, and sang a hymn of thanks for their deliverance.

Years later, André learned from a history professor what happened later on the night they escaped. Right after they fled, the Nazis recognized André's photo in their file and realized he had slipped through their fingers. The Nazi officer who let them escape was sent to the front lines of fighting as punishment for his negligence.

André remained in hiding until just after the Allies landed on the beaches of Normandy, on June 6, 1944. They believed that the victory in Normandy signaled the end of the war and the beginning of a new peace. Although this turned out to be a premature

Arrested Frenchmen are forced from trucks
to cattle cars in Marseille before being
sent to concentration camps.

hope, André and Jacques headed straight for
Le Chambon. Upon their return, Magda, Nelly,
Jean-Pierre, little Daniel, and every member of
the village of Le Chambon met them joyfully.

In André's absence, his spirit had been
maintained in some quarters and forgotten
in others. Le Chambon had grown into an
ever more frequently used stop on the
underground railroad. The Cévenol School

was still a haven for refugees. Édouard Theis, who, like André, was wanted by the Gestapo, had offered his services to the Cimade—a French organization headed by women that assisted Jews and other prisoners fleeing central and eastern Europe—and had begun escorting refugees to the Swiss border.

On the other hand, more young people were joining the Maquis. They were attaching explosives to bridges and train tracks, escalating their levels of violence to match those of the now desperate German troops. The Germans knew the end was near, and sometimes their tactics escalated from murderous to deranged. They shot at civilian vehicles, killed hostages, and threatened to unleash a legion of men trained to kill. In one particularly vicious incident, the village of Oradour-sur-Glane was burned to the ground. The men were shot and the women and children were herded into a church, where they were machine-gunned and set on fire.

The End of the War

Once the Allies landed in the south of France, the Germans were trapped. With no more than a few weeks of war remaining, there were horrible incidents in which German prisoners were murdered by angry, and now victorious, French troops. In Le Chambon, André continued to preach against war and violence to his parishioners and to the 120 German soldiers the Maquis had imprisoned in a castle on the Lignon River. A nation's strength or "rightness" could never entitle it to wage war on another nation.

Many of the Germans still refused to believe that atrocities such as the death camps had ever existed. They clung to the idea of their innocence and hoped that Hitler's armies might still save them from defeat. Many of the maquisards felt that although André's arguments made sense, there was no question that the defeat of the Germans had necessitated violence.

When the soldiers finally departed, André was tired. The horror had ended but, strangely enough, so had some of the joy. The children's houses were closed. Le Chambon, which for five years had been a city of children and committed solidarity, was reverting to its natural dour, granite-faced, taciturn self. Also, André had changed. He had become a leader. No longer simply a local pastor with a strong faith, André was now a proven proponent of nonviolence. He was uniquely positioned, through his work during the war and his skills as a speaker, to preach the message of nonviolence to a larger audience.

Shortly after the war, André became the European secretary of the Fellowship of Reconciliation. He spoke all over Europe and the United States. He also brought attention to the Cévenol School, raising money and interest to sustain it as a center of learning. After a period of work and travel for the Fellowship, André returned to his original calling as pastor in Geneva's parish of Saint-Gervais. While in

A French Resistance fighter stands before the entrance to a crematorium at Natzweiler-Struthof.

Switzerland he remained a pastor until a year before his death, in 1971.

The André Effect

The effectiveness of André Trocmé's influence was based on his ability to inspire and nurture the best in people. He did not tell them what to do. He helped them see what they already believed—about right and wrong and about generosity, the willingness to protect others, and moral goodness. When they understood fully what their consciences told them, André helped them understand that helping was within their personal power.

Much of the violence that occurred during World War II was the result of people's unquestioning submission to authority. Although society will not work if no one obeys its laws, it also fails if no one monitors the convictions and decisions of government leaders. In the first instance, there is chaos. In the second, there is dictatorship. This is what happened in Nazi Germany.

The Nazi government held beliefs that were against the moral conscience, not only of most of the world, but also of most of the German people. Unfortunately, many Germans chose not to protest the government's policies when they disagreed with them.

What happened in Le Chambon was the opposite of unquestioning obedience to authority. André Trocmé may have led the Chambonnais, but he did not dictate. Neighbors rarely knew the extent or nature of each other's rescue efforts. There were some meetings and some collective decisions, but for the most part, each act of resistance was an individual act. André preached that all true responsibility begins with the individual. In Le Chambon, people did not pass on the responsibility of helping those in need to a larger organization. They took the rescue efforts upon themselves, as they understood it in their own minds and hearts.

Looking back at what happened more than half a century later, Magda remarked that had there been an official organization in Le Chambon, it would have failed. The success there came from the absolute sharing of responsibility among everyone. The commitment to protect the refugees in Le Chambon was a consensus, with every individual fully responsible for his or her own actions.

Magda Trocmé (*left*) lights the Eternal Flame at Yad
Vashem in Israel, where she and André were declared
Righteous Among the Nations for their heroic efforts.

Afterword

"The rescue operation that took place in the Plateau Vivaris-Lignon was unique in that it involved the majority of the population of the entire region—Protestant, Catholic, and non-religious—who banded together to carry out what they viewed as their Christian, moral, or political duty. Pastor Trocmé and Mme. Magda Trocmé and Pastor Édouard and Mme. Mildred Theis were among thirty-four residents of the Plateau Vivaris-Lignon who were later recognized by Yad Vashem as Righteous Among the Nations. Eventually, the entire population of the Plateau Vivarais-Lignon was so acknowledged, and a rock garden was planted in their honor in Jerusalem."

—The Holocaust Photo Archives

Timeline

Easter Sunday, 1901 André Trocmé is born.

1914 World War I begins, and the Trocmé home is occupied by Germans.

1921 André joins the French army, where he first demonstrates his principles of nonviolence.

1925 André goes to the United States to work as a French tutor. He meets his future wife, Magda.

January 1933 Adolf Hitler is appointed chancellor of Germany.

March 1933 Hitler assumes dictatorial powers. First concentration camp opens at Dachu.

1934   Hitler becomes commander of the German armed forces. The Trocmés move to Le Chambon.

November 1935   The Nuremberg Laws are passed. Jews are stripped of their rights as German citizens.

November 1938   During *Kristallnacht,* the "Night of Broken Glass," government-organized riots destroy Jewish homes, business, and synagogues.

September 1939   German troops invade Poland, starting World War II.

April 1940   The Auschwitz concentration camp opens.

December 1940   The first German Jewish refugees arrive in Le Chambon for exile.

September 1941   Mass deportations to concentration camps begin. The Nazis round up prisoners as part of *Nacht und Nebel* (Night and Fog) Decree to exterminate the Jews.

January 1942   The Wannsee Conference determines that the Final Solution for the Jewish people is mass extermination.

November 1942   Nazis arrive in Vichy, France and force
the government to hand over
its weapons.

1943   The German Gestapo invades the
Crickets and the House of the Rocks.
André flees his own arrest. André is
arrested along with Édouard Theis and
Roger Darcissac and taken to the
concentration camp of Saint-Paul
d'Eyjeaux. The pastors are freed in a
little more than one month.

1944   Daniel Trocmé is gassed and killed at
the Mardanek death camp in Poland.

June 1944   Allied forces invade Normandy, France.

May 1945   Germany surrenders.

November 1945   The Nuremberg Trials begin.

Glossary

anti-Semitism
Hatred of Jews.

armistice
A temporary suspension of hostilities by mutual
consent; a truce.

Aryan
In Nazi ideology, a person of Germanic background
and member of Hitler's "master race."

atheist
One who does not believe in God.

atrocity
A hideous action or situation.

blitzkrieg
German for "lightning war"; refers to the
combined air and tank attacks perfected by the
Germans during World War II.

communist
One who believes that all the products and power
of a society should be shared equally among its
members.

concentration camp
A prison compound for political prisoners—such
as Jews and communists in Nazi-occupied
France—rather than common criminals.

conscientious objector
One who refuses to serve in the armed forces on
the basis of moral or religious beliefs.

deportation
The forced removal of people from one country or
region to another.

fascist
One who believes in totalitarian government.
Nazism was a form of fascism.

Final Solution
The name of Hitler's plan to kill all the Jews
in Europe.

Gestapo
The Nazi secret police; the name comes from the
German *Geheime Staatspolizei*, which means
"state secret police."

ghetto
An area of a city set aside for a certain group of
  people. For much of European history, there
  were Jewish ghettos in major European cities.

Gospel
The teachings of Jesus Christ as compiled in the
  New Testament of the Bible.

Holocaust
The mass murder of Jews by Nazis during
  World War II.

Nazis
Members of the National Socialist German
  Workers' Party, led by Adolf Hitler.

New Testament
The part of the Bible that includes the story of the
  life of Jesus Christ and Jesus's teachings. After
  Jesus's death, Christians combined the New
  Testament with the Jewish writings of the Old
  Testament to create the Christian Bible.

Old Testament
The part of the Bible that describes God's creation
  of the world and tells the history of the Jews.
  The Old Testament contains Jewish writings
  and the five books of Moses, which are known
  as the Torah.

rationing
The policy of limiting the amount of food allowed to
each individual during wartime or other crises.

refugees
People forced to flee their homes, who seek shelter
elsewhere during wartime or other crises.

resistance
Organized and often secret opposition to a
ruling power.

Treaty of Versailles
Treaty that ended World War I and imposed harsh
terms on Germany.

underground
A network of secret organizations that
facilitate resistance.

Vichy
The city in unoccupied or "free" France that housed
Marshal Henri Pétain's pro-Nazi government.

World War I
A multinational war that lasted from 1914 to 1918.

World War II
A multinational war that lasted from1939 to 1945.

For More Information

Videos

The Holocaust: In Memory of Millions.
Documentary narrated by Walter Cronkite and
produced in 1993.

Night and Fog. Documentary directed by Alain
Resnais and produced in 1955.

Schindler's List. Popular film directed by Steven
Spielberg and produced in 1993.

Survivors of the Holocaust. Documentary
produced in 1995.

*Weapons of the Spirit: The Astonishing Story of a
Unique Conspiracy of Goodness.* Documentary
on Le Chambon. Written and produced by
Pierre Sauvage in 1989.

Web Sites and Organizations

American Society for Yad Vashem
http://www.yadvashem.org

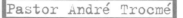

The Cévenol School
http://members.aol.com/lecevenol/usindex.html

Chambon Foundation
http://www.chambon.org

Cybrary of the Holocaust
http://www.remember.org

Historical Timeline on Holocaust Events
http://www.historyplace.com/worldwar2/holocaust/
timeline.html

The Museum of Tolerance
http://www.wiesenthal.com/mot

The Nizkor Project—Holocaust Victims
http://www.nizkor.org

United States Holocaust Memorial Museum
http://www.ushmm.org

For Further Reading

Altshuler, David A. *Hitler's War Against the Jews.* New York: Behrman House, 1978.

Aubrac, Raymond, and Louise Guiney, trans. *The French Resistance: 1940–1944.* Paris, France: Éditions Hazan, 1997.

Frank, Anne. *Diary of a Young Girl: The Definitive Edition.* New York: Bantam Books, 1997.

Hallie, Philip P. *Lest Innocent Blood Be Shed: The Story of the Village of Le Chambon and How Goodness Happened There.* New York: HarperPerennial Library, 1994.

Harris, Mark Jonathan, and Deborah Oppenheimer. *Into the Arms of Strangers: Stories of the Kindertransport.* New York: Bloomsbury, 2000.

Holliday, Laurel, ed. *Children in the Holocaust and World War II: Their Secret Diaries.* New York: Washington Square Press, 1996.

Keneally, Thomas. *Schindler's List.* New York: Simon & Schuster, 1994.

Kustanowitz, Esther. *The Hidden Children of the Holocaust: Teens Who Hid From the Nazis.* New York: The Rosen Publishing Group, 1999.

Matas, Carol. *Daniel's Story.* New York: Simon & Schuster, 1996.

Matas, Carol. *Greater Than Angels.* New York: Simon & Schuster, 1998.

Meltzer, Milton. *Rescue: The Story of How Gentiles Saved Jews in the Holocaust.* New York: Harpercollins, 1991.

Silver, Eric. *The Book of the Just: The Silent Heroes Who Saved Jews from Hitler.* New York: Grove Press, 1992.

Trocmé, André, and Nelly Trocmé, trans. *Angels and Donkeys: Tales for Christmas and Other Times.* Intercourse, PA: Good Books, 1998.

For Advanced Readers

Arendt, Hannah. *The Origins of Totalitarianism.* Rev. ed. New York: Harcourt Brace & Company, 1973.

Camus, Albert, and Stuart Gilbert, trans. *The Plague.* New York: Vintage Books, 1991.

Sweets, John F. *Choices in Vichy France: The French Under Nazi Occupation.* New York: Oxford University Press, 1986.

Index

Acknowledgements

I owe a deep debt of gratitude to the work of historian and philosopher Philip P. Hallie and documentary filmmaker Pierre Sauvage.

About the Author

Allison Stark Draper has written books for younger readers on history, science, and nature. She lives in upstate New York.

Photo Credits

Cover photo © CDJC/Coll,MJDP; p. 4 map by Claudia Carlson; pp. 10, 16, 38, 52 © Hulton Getty Archive; pp. 22, 25, 79 © Peter Feigl, courtesy of USHMM Photo Archives; pp. 26, 72 © Jacqueline Gregory, courtesy of USHMM Photo Archives; pp. 30, 50, 93 © National Archives, courtesy of USHMM Photo Archives; p. 34 © Hulton-Deustch Collection/Corbis; p. 42 © Philip Hallie, courtesy of USHMM Photo Archives; p. 58 © Hanna Meyer-Moses, courtesy of USHMM Photo Archives; p. 61 © Robert Trocmé, courtesy of USHMM Photo Archives; pp. 63, 96 © Yad Vashem Photo Archives, courtesy of USHMM Photo Archives; p. 68 © Corbis Bettmann; p. 89 © Bundesarchiv.

Series Design
Cynthia Williamson

Layout
Les Kanturek